inspired

C.S. LEWIS

About Wyatt North Publishing

Starting out with just one writer, Wyatt North Publishing has expanded to include writers from across the country. Our writers include college professors, religious theologians, and historians.

Wyatt North Publishing provides high quality, perfectly formatted, original books.

Send us an email and we will personally respond within 24 hours! As a boutique publishing company we put our readers first and never respond with canned or automated emails. Send us an email at hello@WyattNorth.com, and you can visit us at www.WyattNorth.com.

Foreword

A man of reason and vigorous discourse, and a renowned professor of literature and philosophy, C.S. Lewis, always "Jack" to family and friends, never shied from intellectual debate, and through his written works encouraged others to wrestle with the difficult questions of faith.

A master of visual illustration and allegory, Lewis wrote with the intuitive understanding that his readers wrestled with the same questions about the Christian story, about pain, suffering, and notions of Heaven and Hell, as he himself had wrestled. He also understood that others found reason and imagination to be incompatible aspects of an understanding of God and the universe.

Table of Contents

An Introduction

"I am a product of long corridors, empty sunlit rooms, upstairs indoor silences, attics explored in solitude...Also, of endless books..."

Clive Staples Lewis, born in Belfast, Ireland at the end of the nineteenth century and "dragged, kicking and screaming, into the [Christian] faith" would prove to be not only one of the most influential and widely-read Christian theologians of the twentieth century, but one whose prolific writings continue to enthrall, irritate, provoke, and inspire readers to this day. A man of reason and vigorous discourse, and a renowned professor of literature and philosophy, C.S. Lewis, always "Jack" to family and friends, never shied from intellectual debate, and through his written works encouraged others to wrestle with the difficult questions of faith. A master of visual illustration and allegory, Lewis wrote with the intuitive understanding that his readers wrestled with the same questions about the Christian story, about pain, suffering, and notions of Heaven and Hell, as he himself had wrestled. He also understood that others found reason and imagination to be incompatible aspects of an understanding of God and the universe.

Lewis was a cerebral type, skilled at building logical arguments, and large in personality. A professor known for a booming voice which often built up steam as he entered a lecture hall, his lecture already well underway, Lewis, through his teachings, inspired—no, demanded—consideration of the world as one assumed it to be, and consideration as to whether what one perceived was, indeed, the truth. Outside the university setting of Oxford and the books he published in his professional field, his writings would not only receive waves of public response and help readers take a good look at their faith or lack of one, but would also serve as a lens turned mindfully inwards to the workings of Lewis' own musings, which he shared. Once settled in his Christian convictions after a circuitous migration through several different philosophical doctrines, Lewis admitted in his autobiographical book *Surprised by Joy* that "most of [my] books are evangelistic," from his apologetic writings to his works of fiction for adults and children. (Here in this text, any quotations not noted otherwise come from this same volume, whose title reveals much about the way Lewis arrived at faith, as we shall see.) Today, though still respected for his entire body of published work, Lewis is often associated with the fictional series he wrote for children, that of the Chronicles of Narnia, a series whose timelessness illustrates the author's singular talents.

Talent attracts critics and scrutiny, however, and this series, along with the modern movies made from them, spark debate to this day, a legacy which also testifies to the durability of Lewis' storytelling. Something in the writings of Narnia still resonates strongly, though today's readers are of an era quite unlike the war years and Oxford mindset of which Lewis himself was a product. Criticized in his own time for both an unorthodox style of crafting fiction—the mixing of elements of mythology with Christian allegory was positively scandalous to Lewis' friend J.R.R. Tolkien—and for the enthusiasm of his apologetic works which brought embarrassment to his professional peers, and criticized in modern times for the hints of misogyny and racism that some examiners find in his works, Lewis nonetheless produced a prolific body of work throughout his career inside and outside of the university, adding to the significant contributions to both the Christian faith and the field in which he taught, that of English literature.

Were he alive today, C.S. Lewis might offer us a reminder of one essential tenet that unites the entire body of his lifetime's work: that in examination of a thing, it is possible to lose sight of the thing itself. If modern readers can step beyond the lenses of their own era and the scrutinizing subjectivity of individual perspective, and are able to strip away the distractions of Lewis' own personality and temporal prejudices, then they'll see the Narnian forest for the trees. Above all else, Lewis' legacy has helped many readers to recognize the great joy that transcends all time, denominations, and limitations of human mind, and to simply become aware of the delightful presence of a loving, everlasting God.

Childhood Happiness and First Tastes of Joy

There's a certain irony in the fact that Lewis, who never had children of his own nor seems to have been particularly fond of spending time around them, is today most often associated with the Narnian fantasy series. But it was in books that Lewis himself had some of his earliest childhood experiences of joy, a sensation that encapsulates the whole experience of the presence of God, and which, by Lewis' description, is an altogether different experience from either happiness or pleasure— and key to all relationships with the divine. *Surprised by Joy*, candid in its personal revelations, offers an openness quite unlike the author's personality in real life, in which he was notably private about personal affairs.

Born in 1898 to Albert and Flora Lewis, "Jack" grew up among the sweeping views of hill and coastline of County Down in Ireland, though many of those early rainy Irish days were spent indoors in a house of modest size and modest garden, a period of "humdrum, prosaic happiness" punctuated by "moments of joy" with days spent in the company of elder brother Warren, called "Warnie," four years Jack's senior. The brothers created a play-haven of sorts in their indoor playroom that looked out over the Castlereagh Hills, the hills beckoning from far beyond the rain. Young Jack, content to sit for days on end drawing an invented place called Animal Land, entertained himself with a world of fantasy illustrations, which by today's standard might be considered imaginative play, though Lewis firmly refuted that this world of sketches was "imaginative" at all. In fact, in works written many decades later in life, Lewis would use the creatures of Animal Land to illustrate the distinction between what is "made" by a creator, and what is "begat," a concept we will explore further on.

Jack's Animal Land took shape alongside his brother's tales of an imagined "India" until the brothers merged their separate play-realms into a new place called Boxen, a world where adventures would hover somewhere between nostalgia and anticipation of renewing the hobby throughout both brothers' lives. In its simple way, the blending of Animal Land and India foreshadowed what would later become a uniting theme of Lewis' career: that dichotomies weren't always what they seemed, and that realms could overlap. But more on this later. What is essential to note about those early years is that, somewhere around age seven, Jack Lewis experienced three distinct bursts of awe— moments from "another dimension"— which would linger in his memory and form the earliest threads of true "joy" as he himself defined it; an ache, from the soul's deep longing to know that which— beyond the physical, temporal realm— has created it. So powerful were the sensations that Lewis insists that, "the reader who finds these three episodes of no interest need read this book no further, for in a sense the central story of [my] life is about nothing else."

First among these was a fleeting incident, experienced while playing outdoors, of a toy garden built in a biscuit tin by Warnie; a moment Lewis noted at the time for not only its delight, but for the intense desire left in the passing moment's wake, and also the ensuing confusion as to what exactly the object of such longing really was for—surely it wasn't for the old biscuit tin garden itself? Even at such a young age, Lewis recognized the way the memory-moment calling from "hundreds of years away" had made the commonplace world fall away, and saw that what he hungered for was for some other quality of the toy his brother had built, not for the tin full of soil and tiny plants itself. What he wanted was the want itself; that was the "unsatisfied desire...more desirable than any other satisfaction." Yet "It had taken only a moment of time; and in a certain sense everything else that had ever happened to me was insignificant in comparison."

The second and third incidents, though they came through two quite dissimilar books, incited similar longing through their passages of natural imagery, both moving Lewis to thumb the books' pages again and again in attempt to reawaken and savor this feeling of joy.

First of these was Beatrix Potter's *Squirrel Nutkin*, which brought both a crush and a confusion in Jack, who wanted "to know autumn—[but also] to possess autumn; but how can one possess a season?" Whatever the particulars of fall imagery that appealed to him, autumn, that season in which life squeezes itself into a nutshell and succumbs to the inevitability of winter and subsequent rebirth, appealed to a reader too young to recognize at that time how so simple an allegory would encapsulate faith itself and remain the major quest of his spiritual life. (Incidentally, Lewis treasured the story and respected its author always, holding Beatrix Potter in high esteem even late in his life. Unfortunately, he narrowly missed his chance to meet her at her home, Potter passing away just before Lewis had opportunity to take a trip to England's Lake District where she lived.) Talking animals—so simple and common to the modern reader that we forget what a novelty they were at the time the Peter Rabbit stories were written—caught his interest and held it even as, as gifted children often do, Jack skipped much of the works written for children and leaped right into the world of literature for adults.

The third experience, when Lewis was a young teen and fascinated with everything Norse, from the heroic tragedy of its mythology to Wagner's music, came from an excerpt of Longfellow's *Saga of King Olaf* describing the tragic end of the dying god Balder the Beautiful, in which the sky itself—"cold, spacious, severe, pale, and remote"—birthed a yearning surpassing the biscuit tin and Beatrix Potter experiences: "...I desired with almost sickening intensity something never to be described." Even as a teen Lewis recognized—and lamented—his inability to put verbal parameters around that which stirred something inside him. Something in this celestial, eternal theme attached itself to the horizon of Lewis' mind, and refused to set as childhood was put to bed.

The End of Reliability and Tranquility

Trickles of grief from that "cold, spacious" sky rained down on the Lewis brothers' childhood with the demise of their mother Flora, not long after the family had moved from their modest house overlooking the hills to a much grander house in the countryside—an enormous, poorly built dwelling stuffed with reading material: "Endless books...There were books in the study, books in the drawing room, books in the cloakroom, books (two deep) in the great bookcase on the landing, books piled high as my shoulder in the cistern attic, books of all kinds reflecting every transient stage of my parents' interest, books readable and unreadable, books suitable for a child and books most emphatically not. Nothing was forbidden me...I always had the same certainty of finding a book that was new to me as a man who walks into a field has of finding a new blade of grass." This sprawling library would shelter Jack and Warnie throughout the scarring experiences of their mother's diagnosis with cancer, her operation (exploratory surgeries were performed at home in those days), her sickroom confinement and death, the viewing of her body, and funeral—frightful experiences for a child, which remained in the author's mind as he wrote for children in later years. It was during this ordeal, which others have tried to describe as Lewis' first religious experience and which he insists otherwise— that Lewis first spoke to God in prayer, though the disappointment that followed when God failed to deliver a miracle didn't deal a devastating blow of any sort. As an adult Lewis explained this seeming contradiction, saying that, "He [God] was, in my mental picture...merely a magician," and not a very talented one at that. A faith as "irreligious" as his was at that time didn't count.

Upon Flora's demise, Albert caved to grief and a tendency towards erratic, unpredictable behavior and "wild words" which caused the relationship between father and sons to grow distant. The boys clung to each other, Lewis and Warnie to their own devices with not only that particular grief of children which Lewis addresses as equal but different to the grief of adult, but also the noises and whisperings of that drafty house of echoes, drains that gurgled, and winds that howled. All that was "reliable and tranquil" had disappeared. The cold, cavernous setting left its imprint on Lewis' psyche; it became, as he remarked in later years, "almost a major character of my books." With clipped precision in a quick autobiographical list of personal attributes, Lewis admits that: "Alone in a big house full of books...I suppose that fixed a literary bent."

The years following the death of his mother, who had been highly educated herself in a time when many women weren't and who had taken a first-class degree in logic plus a second in mathematics, passed for Lewis as a cloud of general dislike for- and at times outright animosity and rebellion against- the schools he attended. Following in Warnie's footsteps at preparatory school, Lewis floundered. Where Warnie had excelled at sports and games and had mastered the complicated social structure of snobbery and not-uncommon brutality, Jack was picked on by what he called the "Bloods," the prefect students who were allowed to haze boys not considered good at sports. (Lewis was, apparently, rather clumsy). Such actions were allowed, even sanctioned, in the school culture at that time, and Jack despised it.

In the autumn of 1914, Lewis' pleas to his father to rescue him from his place of torment were heard, and arrangements were made for Jack to be sent away to England for schooling instead, to live in the home and under the care and tutelage of William T. Kirkpatrick, a family friend and former headmaster who had not only taught Albert, but had also taken Warnie some years before, as a private student (Warnie was not quite as academically gifted as Jack) to help prepare him for entry to Sandhurst military academy. Dubbed "Kirk,"— also "The Great Knock," "Old Knock," or simply "Knock," Kirkpatrick would not only educate the younger Lewis brother in whom he saw a tremendous gift for language, but mold the boy's nimble mind into a powerhouse of reason, logic, and argumentation, which would guide Lewis' thought processes for the rest of his life.

The Great Knock

"If ever a man came near to being a purely logical entity," Lewis claims, "that man was Kirk." An Ulster Scot who had discarded Presbyterianism in favor of an Atheist view, Kirk, along with his oft-chagrined wife who cooked and cared for Jack and taught him French, proved to be a vigorous—and vigorously unorthodox—teacher fond of surprises and abhorrent of excess chatter. At the very first meeting of teacher and student, the latter of whom had expected years of politesse and formal discourse, Jack received a shock: "Stop!" shouted Kirk, startling his new pupil, who had made a casual remark about the "wildness" of Bookham upon arrival. The landscape was not as he'd pictured. Kirk gave a shout, "What do you mean by wildness, and what grounds had you for not expecting it?" The minutes and years of debate that followed—with Kirk always demanding sound argument and justification for any claims made— shaped a reliance on proof, evidence, and realism, with similar interrupting outbursts of "Stop!" and "Go on," punctuating all of Lewis' three years at Bookham as a pupil. In addition to this insistence on skillful discourse and sound argument, Kirk demanded a high standard of self-guided reading, of constant challenge, comparison, and evaluation of the great classics of literature, always read in their original languages. No watering down of the great stories of Homer or Horace was to be had; Kirk would brook no degradation of the majesty of such wonderful works, and made Lewis learn the languages in which they had been written.

It is interesting to note that several of Kirk's quirks would later serve to refine Lewis' much-later adoption of Christian faith, though they were intended to reinforce his own philosophy of the Rationalist Atheism common in that era. One statement in particular seems particularly relevant, made by the teacher at that first meeting: "Do you not see, then, that you had no right to have any opinion whatever on the subject?" Though this remark had referred merely to the landscape of Surrey, it encapsulates the whole of Lewis' reaction at his first encounter, many years later, with God, when he realized, as philosophies and rationales fell away like ill-fitting, discarded hats, that he'd had an immature understanding of the subject. With thanks falling obliquely to Kirk, Lewis would, when he finally got it, arrive at faith fully informed and deserving of an opinion upon it.

Among Knock's other gifts to Lewis were an insistence upon the constant improvement and refinement of one's inner workings—a learning curve, set seemingly unattainably high at times—and a willingness to listen, though Knock himself was not as inclined to listen as he was keen to point out any holes he perceived in the statements of others. Lewis mentions, "I hear you" as the closest thing to praise ever uttered by Kirk, who became a father figure of sorts when Lewis' relationship with his own was disintegrating.

It is interesting to note here the widely differing perceptions that Lewis and his father had of the same teacher, with Albert claiming Knock to be an affectionate, comforting sort of man who freely bestowed gentle praise on his students, and Jack Lewis looking back on his time with Knock as a learning experience full of intellectual "tossings" and "knock downs"— though he also admits he enjoyed the treatment as it forced him to put on intellectual muscle. Perhaps the discrepancy was due to a gap in years, or simply personality; whatever the case, it may have influenced Lewis' later writings on the differences between Christian denominations— that Anglicans, Methodists, Baptists, and Presbyterians, and all others were simply "different rooms within the same house." Arguments between them, he said, only served to drive anyone interested in that house far away. In the Body of Christ, an ear had no business saying the eye was perceiving things wrongly. Differences were, as we shall see later, an essential part of God's diversity, a theme Lewis illustrated at the end of the Narnia series.

But back to his teenage years, and Lewis' adopted belief in the same atheist rationalism as his tutor: "Some boys would not have liked it; to me it was red beef and strong beer." A hearty education indeed! "Kirk excited and satisfied one side of me," Lewis explains, and that was the proof-loving, evidence-demanding view of the universe and everything in it. With the intellectual bar set high during those years studying under Kirk, Lewis rose to the challenge, vowing to never again allow himself to take a "child's head" view of anything. And all future inquiries and acceptances would be guided by this modus operandi. "God is no fonder of intellectual slackers than of any other slackers," he writes in *Mere Christianity*, many years later. "If you are thinking of becoming a Christian, I warn you, you are embarking on something which is going to take the whole of you, brains and all."

Lewis does also mention one clue that, perhaps, though his teacher lived by it and passed it on, Old Knock's "brains and all" approach wasn't quite as wholly embraced as the man with a "grip…like iron pincers" claimed, for Knock, an Ulster Scot, retained one inexplicable quirk, as though he couldn't quite shake off the cloak of his Presbyterian upbringing entirely: The teacher always wore his Sunday best clothing when gardening on the Sabbath.

A Sense of Reverence Even in Disbelief

Jack had abandoned all belief in anything Christian, as well as the dutiful motions he had performed—and grown to resent—throughout his childhood in the Anglican Church, but had become enthralled by tales of heroic myth. The Christ story, he decided, was every bit as beautiful, heroic, and false as the Norse myths, just another good story along the lines of that tragic —if moving— scene involving Balder the Beautiful, another God-story invented by the ancients and following the same pagan themes of death and rebirth, themes with obvious origins in the seasonality of agriculture.

Perhaps it is fair here to note that Atheism, in Lewis' time, was a bit more like Agnosticism now, not so much an anti-God rhetoric as a discarding of belief in favor of a pessimistic view of life. How could a world so full of sorrow and suffering have room for a loving God? Where was there any proof? "Had I any evidence in my own experience?" Interestingly, it was around this time that Lewis went through confirmation at the church near his home town, St. Mark's, Dundela, to avoid making waves with his father, to whom Lewis could not bring himself to yet admit his disbelief in Christianity. Lewis thus professed his beliefs publicly and dishonestly, an act he abhorred later in life as one of the worst things he ever did.

Jack studied Greek, Latin, Italian, German, and French and the literatures original to these, reveling in not only his escape from the horrible school he had attended previously, but in the freedom given him to commune with books, and indulge his love of them so freely. Outside of the classics, Kirkpatrick generally allowed Lewis to choose his own self-guided reading once his student demonstrated that the choices would be educationally sound, and academically Lewis flourished. All his pocket money went to ordering books by post, and he began to take interest in other genres: Poetry and verse; romantic writings which his parents hadn't had much taste for, and works concerned with the land of Faery. This is not to say Lewis developed an interest in fairies as we think of them today; rather, there was and is, in the more Celtic-influenced areas, a lasting lore about another realm which paralleled that of visible Britain. Faery and its inhabitants were neither inherently good, nor bad; they could be both tempting, beneficial, and cruel.

One particular work—read, interestingly, at Knock's behest—was a work by George MacDonald called *Phantastes*, an assignment that would later add kindling to Lewis' faith—an effect quite opposite of what Knock, in assigning it, had presumably intended. The book would, as Lewis puts it, "baptize" his imagination. Lewis became mesmerized by the book, fascinated by its overriding theme of reverence—of something holy, something worth longing for. Naturally, this resonated strongly with Lewis and his early tastes of and quests for joy.

In *Phantastes*, reality didn't have to be based on reason. There was a quality, "the quality of the real universe, the divine, magical, terrifying, and ecstatic reality in which we all live," that Lewis loved. Though Jack was put off at that time by MacDonald's faith, the only irksome quality of an author held otherwise in high esteem, "George MacDonald (did) more to (me) than any other writer; of course it was a pity he had that bee in his bonnet about Christianity."

Faith was still years away, much too far of a chasm to bridge, though Lewis did love to indulge that side of his brain that craved imaginative thought as much as he loved to exercise that half which adored sound reasoning. What we might nowadays call "right" and "left" brain were still separate, each side "pure," not to be mixed. But an internal battle kept nagging at his thoughts: "Nearly all that I loved I believed to be imaginary; nearly all that I believed to be real I thought grim and meaningless."

One of Lewis' favorite aspects of daily life at Bookham were his walks in the Surrey countryside. County Down, his Ireland home, had been wide horizons and open views of the sea; Surrey was full of "contours...the little valleys so narrow, there was so much timber, so many villages concealed in woods or hollows...such an unpredictable variety...that the whole thing could never lie clearly in my mind, and to walk in it daily gave one the same sort of pleasure that there is in the labyrinthine complexity of...the *Faerie Queen* [by Edmund Spenser.]" Clearly the young atheist still had something of the romantic inside. Walking through Surrey on school days and through his home territory on holidays, Lewis says "[their] beauties were such that even a fool could not force them into competition, [and] this cured me once and for all of the pernicious tendency to compare and prefer."

Thus an appreciation for beauty, at least of the natural world, remained. Lewis held Kirk in highest esteem, indebted to the man for the rest of his career, as the man who "excited and satisfied" that rational half of his mind. "My debt to him is very great, my reverence to this day undiminished."

Battles of More Than the Mind

In 1917 Lewis left the Kirkpatricks' care, and was accepted on scholarship to study at University College of Oxford, where he intended to begin a course of study in Greek and Latin Literature. However, after only five months, World War I had broken out, and Britain was at war. Lewis enlisted in the British Army and was sent for officer training, where he befriended his roommate E.C.F. "Paddy" Moore, and found himself on the front lines in the Somme Valley of France on his nineteenth birthday. Exploding shells, endless mud, deep bunkers...The numbing imagery and gore of battle would haunt a whole generation of young men—or at least those who survived. Paddy did not.

Lewis kept a promise made to Paddy to look after Paddy's mother, Janie Moore, and sister Maureen; after the war was over Lewis would live with them from 1921 until Mrs. Moore's death. (The nature of Lewis' relationship with Mrs. Moore, whom he called "Minto" and who was old enough to be his mother, has been the source of much speculation, sometimes said to be romantic, sometimes said to be a surrogate parent/son relationship. Whatever it was precisely, further speculation is beyond the scope of this book. There is, however, one curious glimpse of Lewis' personality revealed in it, as the relationship— or rather, the hold Mrs. Moore held on Lewis, keeping him at her beck and call throughout his school and professional career— was one subject Lewis absolutely refused to discuss with anyone, even his own brother and father, who were concerned at the way Lewis spent much of his allowance in supporting the mother and daughter pair. Lewis only reluctantly acknowledged, and flatly refused to discuss, the nature of his relationship with this staunchly atheist, not at all intellectual older woman. In later years, Moore became a burden upon Lewis, requiring a great deal of care, with her confined to bed in her last years, yet remaining persnickety over care of her pet dog Bruce and over management of the household. Hiring nurses and housekeepers to look after her so that he could attend to work placed heavy demands on Lewis during his professional years, and either forced or honed an innate talent for focusing sharply and writing with high productivity in what meager free time he had.)

Wounded in battle, Lewis spent his hospital recovery time putting to ink a series of lyric poems he'd been working on during quieter times in the trenches, poems which reveal some turbulent emotions. Collectively called *Spirits in Bondage*, the tales of giants and faeries and the old heroic Gods reveal a fear: Lewis was afraid that the imaginative "half" of the world was dying. Anger, loss, a sense that joy was fading out of reach...Lewis at this point was mourning more than fallen friends. He was mourning something within himself that was ailing.

One would assume that the trauma of this Great War would leave its ghastly imprint not only on the mind and spirit, but also on the works Lewis would write in years to come, but this isn't always freely shared with his readers. In his works written for children it is easy to understand why he keeps gory scenes to a minimum (e.g. "Horrible things were happening wherever she [Lucy] looked," and "The children did not see the actual moment of the killing" from *The Lion, The Witch, and The Wardrobe*) but Lewis was intensely private with emotions. Even a volume written after the death of his wife in his older years, *A Grief Observed*, is relatively terse and was released under a pseudonym. Lewis was reluctant to offer autobiographical details if they lay beyond the scope of mental matters. What is readily apparent is that, after Lewis was wounded by shrapnel and taken to a hospital to convalesce, his mind was still locked in a battlefield of its own. Lewis' father Albert, though he was written with a request to do so, did not come to visit his son; the relationship had deteriorated badly.

His response to a friend who asked "Were you much frightened in France?" could have stemmed from soldier's stoicism, a lingering insistence on rationalism, or outright honesty— or even a mix of all three—but whatever was behind it, Lewis answered with, "All the time, but I never sank so low as to pray."

A Return to Oxford

In January of 1919, with war over and the waves of soldiers that had flooded the campus ebbed away, Lewis returned to the "dreaming spires" of Oxford and all its delightful offerings: libraries full of old books, smoky cafes, winding streets of architecture. This time, finishing his course of study in Greek and Latin Literature, Lewis tacked on courses (degrees) in Philosophy and Ancient History, and also, when he was not yet able to find a teaching position, English.

Prior to Oxford, Lewis had delighted in regimented, self-reliant study and endless reading, with meals and tea brought at regular intervals on trays, and those long rambling walks in the afternoons—"Epicurean" days, such as he had enjoyed at Bookham. Lewis felt—always—that walks were best taken alone, or at least with companions who didn't talk much, as "[walking] and talking are two very great pleasures, but it is a mistake to combine them. Our own noise blots out the sounds and silences of the outdoor world." (Each apparently spoiled enjoyment of the other. Quite amusingly to the modern reader, Lewis felt that conversation led "inevitably" to smoking, and thus a subsequent loss of the scents of nature. Tea, too, was best taken in one's own company.) At Oxford, though, Lewis began to gradually unfold himself and open up to making new acquaintances. Known generally as a man who kept to himself and was often seen leaving campus on his bicycle, Lewis was made fun of for being a messenger, with only a few of his closest companions ever learning where he went, which was to Mrs. Moore's house. (In time, those friends found a way to "accidentally" meet the elusive woman, whom Lewis was by no means eager to introduce. At that time, students were required to live in their assigned lodging, returning before curfew each evening; Lewis got away with much of his time off-campus since, with the flood of soldiers returning and swelling the Oxford undergraduate population, there had been arrangements made for some to live further away. Thus, his comings and goings didn't stand out as much as they might have otherwise.)

In time he collected and delighted in a wider social circle of friends, peers who shared his appetite for intellectual thinking, heady debate, and the exchange of ideas, but two friends met at Oxford would particularly engage Lewis, challenging him to philosophical duels in the same way as had Old Knock, who passed away in 1921. Lewis, ever excited by the exchange of ideas, embraced those who were his equal in argumentative agility and verbal sparring.

First of these friends was Owen Barfield, a fellow student who, like Lewis, would also eventually become an Oxford professor. In the first years of a friendship that would last their lifetimes, the two men formed a relationship which Lewis humorously calls their own personal "Great War," an ongoing conversational debate that was never an outright quarrel but an "incessant disputation." Even when not in one another's company, the two friends kept it going via written correspondence. (Lewis also kept up a similar correspondence with one of his few childhood friends, Arthur Greaves, who had been a devout Christian, just as Lewis was choosing atheism. The two friends agreed to disagree. Years later, though, the very justifications Greaves offered became the very position Lewis would propose to the wider world.)

Barfield had embraced a way of thinking called anthroposophy, the philosophy of spiritual science put forth by Rudolph Steiner a few decades before, which held that there had been a major rift, widening since the Middle Ages, between the natural sciences, the arts, and man's own spiritual yearning. Though anthroposophy defined itself as neither a religious faith nor a precursor to one, it nonetheless failed to appeal to Lewis, who defended the realist views he had formed before arriving at school. But Barfield gets credit for dealing Lewis' love of pure logic two wounding blows: one to "chronological snobbery," the other to the view that the universe can be explained by the five senses alone.

Firstly, Barfield helped Lewis to see that just because one's generation and its accompanying body of literature were steeped in a popular idea or philosophy, that didn't mean that the philosophies of the past were wrong. He forced Lewis to acknowledge the necessity of examining why they came and went: Had the older schools of thought been proved wrong, or could truth be found in something that had gone out of style? Just because a thing or idea had become passé didn't mean it ought to be discarded wholesale.

Barfield's second blow forced the issue of the meaning of "mind." If Lewis were determined to keep clinging to realism, then he had to accept that "thought" itself, as a product of cumulative and inherited input from the five senses, was a relatively new phenomenon in the universe, since it came with the advent of humans. Lewis would also thus need to embrace the Theory of Behaviorism, which insisted that there is no such thing as "mind" at all, only behavior, since behavior, not mind, could be measured and studied. The concept of "mind" had no proof, but actions did. Of behaviorism, Lewis said later he could no more have accepted it than he could have scratched his ear with his own big toe.

Forced to acknowledge that he did indeed believe in something greater—a mind at the back of things, which he refers to as a sort of "cosmic logos"—the young adult Lewis still wasn't ready to admit that there was anything particularly theistic about this larger mind of the universe at all. It could exist, but that didn't necessarily mean it was synonymous with God. "I suspect there was some willful blindness," Lewis later writes about this period of his spiritual journey. "I wanted Nature to be something...indifferent."

Forced to accede to Barfield's point, Lewis embraced the idea of the absolute mind, though he kept it as the idea of something larger than human thought but which posed "no danger of Its doing anything about us. It was "there"; safely and immovably "there." It would never come "here," never (to be blunt) make a nuisance of Itself...There was nothing to fear; better still, nothing to obey." Lewis was only willing to accept that, indeed, reason alone was not enough to either understand or to use as a tool to contemplate either logic or ethics or the complex nature of the universe. There had to be something larger, something absolute, a mind that established that basic human notion of right and wrong that lurked at the back of every discussion of morality. Our own mind, the very tool we use to examine mind, was a product of the mind itself; this revelation presented a sticky wicket which could not be bypassed.

"And so the great Angler played His fish," Lewis says of this development, "and I never dreamed that the hook was in my tongue."

A Bee in Several Bonnets

The other notable acquaintance Lewis made at Oxford was one recognized as a great friend right from the first words they exchanged in an English class, when Lewis began the additional course of study in that department: "And there I made a new friend. The very first words he spoke marked him out from the ten or twelve others who were present; a man after my own heart..." Note that Lewis uses the word heart, not mind. And their minds certainly differed; Neville Coghill, a brilliant student, was Christian. "I soon had the shock," Lewis reveals, "of discovering that he—clearly the most intelligent and best-informed man in that class-was a Christian and thorough-going supernaturalist." Shock, indeed. How could someone so informed choose to accept something so implausible as that mythology of Jesus Christ? Naturally, the two friends vigorously debated their views.

Coghill chipped further away at that "chronological snobbery" whose legitimacy Barfield had begun to poke holes in, reiterating that there might still be truths to be found in the older ways of thinking—and "older" certainly fit the climate of Oxford at that time; unbelief was the norm, the study of divinity merely perfunctory to education. Lewis writes about the gradual abandoning of this unbelief in *Mere Christianity*: "My argument against God was that the universe seemed so cruel and unjust. But how had I got this idea of just and unjust? A man does not call a line crooked unless he has some idea of a straight line…Consequently atheism turns out to be too simple. If the whole universe has no meaning, we should never have found out that it has no meaning; just as, if there were no light in the universe and therefore no creatures with eyes, we should never know it was dark." He wondered, in *Surprised by Joy*, "Had something really dropped out of our lives?"

Looking back over the works of his favorite authors of many eras at about this same time, Lewis began to feel that they all had a quality in common, something he says allowed him to "trust [them] utterly," though he wasn't quite sure why. MacDonald, Johnson, Spencer, Milton… all had accepted this Christian way of thinking, too. Even the ancient writers of Greece and Rome whose epic adventures Lewis admired all had something in common, a religious bent, pre-Christian though it was. Could even these pre-Christian writers have had a glimpse of a truth that was to arrive later in time? On the contrary, Voltaire, Shaw, Wells, authors who "did not suffer from religion" began to seem to Lewis "a little thin; what as boys we called 'tinny.'…There seemed to be no depth in them. They were too simple. The roughness and density of life did not appear in their books." A dissatisfaction was growing; one imagines the beginnings of a humming in Lewis' ear, insisting on being named either tinnitus, or the same "bee in the bonnet" that whispered to the writers he admired.

"All the books were beginning to turn against me," Lewis wrote of this discomfort. "Indeed, I must have been blind as a bat not to have seen, long before, the ludicrous contradiction between my theory of life and my actual experiences as a reader." Not yet taking what would seem the obvious next step of giving this faith of those who he respected a thorough and immediate investigation, Lewis did begin to allow himself to be labeled a theist, as one who believed that the great absolute mind behind all the universe might indeed be a God of sorts. He still was not at all keen at allowing that God to step in any closer than arm's length and "interfere."

The Inklings

Just as Lewis was taking those first steps along the path of contemplation of the existence of a Heavenly Father, his earthly one died. The event, combined with the erosion of those naturalist beliefs he'd held onto for years, pushed Lewis to do what he had never done outside a sense of duty: In the spring term of 1929, Lewis finally "gave in, and admitted God was God, and knelt and prayed…"

The passing of Lewis, Sr. in September of that year was followed by another surprise: the permanent return of Warnie to the Anglican Church the brothers had been raised in. Though their relationship never reverted to the cozy companionship the two had enjoyed early on—in those days when they sat and conjured up imaginary worlds— the grown Lewis men would always remain united by their shared, strained relationship with their biological father, and managed to piece together a functional, if at times harmonious only in outward appearance, dynamic that supported one another through adulthood. (Warnie would become, in the following years, a regular member of the group of friends discussed below, as well as another respected opinion on the subject of faith. He was also of great help to Lewis, acting as an assistant of sorts, though as the years progressed and Warnie retired and moved in with Lewis and Mrs. Moore, Warnie's alcoholism would become yet another domestic trial with which the busy writer had to cope.)

As his career as Professor of literature began (English as a field was still in its beginnings, viewed as a somewhat vague field of study, and not very masculine in comparison with study of the classics, or history), Lewis' social interactions widened still further, and a group of literary friends, who called themselves "the Inklings" formed—quite an appropriate name, suggesting both the physical liquid medium of the written word, as well as the glimmer of ideas. In a later short description of himself, Lewis says "My happiest hours are spent with three or four old friends in old clothes tramping [hiking] together and putting up in small pubs—or else sitting up till the small hours in someone's college rooms talking nonsense, poetry, theology, metaphysics over beer, tea, and pipes. There's no sound I like better than adult male laughter."

The Inklings held weekly meetings in a pub called The Eagle and Child, referred to affectionately by the group's members as the "Bird and Baby." These weekly, if not more frequent gatherings, would last for sixteen years, and it was through interactions and debates held in the fellowship of this group— all writers, all male, all of whom shared an enthusiasm for fantasy literature and narrative— that faith finally left the page for Lewis and became a living, animated thing. Lewis' perceptions of Christianity were greatly influenced by two Inklings members, his friends J.R.R. Tolkien and Hugo Dyson. It was after a walk with these two men in 1931 and a discussion of metaphor and myth, that Lewis first wrote acknowledgement of his newfound belief. The two men would "give [me] much help in getting over the last stile."

As we have seen, Lewis had discounted the specifics of the Christian story as being too similar to those ancient pagan themes of death and resurrection—in other words, just another heroic myth, with all the imagery taken from the cycles of their natural surroundings. Tolkien and Dyson convinced Lewis that, rather then discrediting the experience of Jesus Christ, the ancient tales actually proved its veracity, because the old tales showed that the pagans thousands of years before had seen a glimpse of its truth, of the reality that was to come with the Savior's arrival. And rather than offering the same cyclical imagery of the seasonal year, this story had a one-time-only place in datable history. Unlike the pagan tales of dying and reincarnating gods, this one had ties to time and geographical space, connections to the physical world. And that made all the difference.

Thus, for the first time, reason and imagination were able to co-exist peacefully in Lewis' mind. He describes the actual moment of connection of these realms of reason and imagination as having taken place the morning after that fateful walk with Tolkien and Dyson, a moment that took place on a motorcycle ride to the Whipsnade Zoo with his brother. "When we set out I did not believe that Jesus Christ was the Son of God, and when we reached the zoo I did." A reconciliation of mind— of art and science, in a way— had taken place.

Joy Becomes More Than a Longing

Joy, it seemed, had finally arrived, with explanations for itself. Those early childhood experiences of intense longing came back to Lewis, in the sense that the object of all those longings was now recognized as one and the same: the Creator Itself. Previously, Lewis had understood—and felt keenly—what it was like to *want* to experience bliss, but its target remained tragic and murky. And those moments of bliss disappeared as soon as one became aware of the experience—as soon as the moment was thought about, it was gone, leaving ache in its wake. One couldn't have one's bliss and analyze it, too.

"Joy itself, considered simply as an event in my own mind, turned out to be of no value at all. All the value lay in that of which Joy was the desiring. And that object, quite clearly, was no state of my own mind or body at all." Even as a youngster Lewis had been aware that it wasn't the toy tin garden built by his brother that he craved; it was the *joy* of remembering the toy that had brought such pleasure, and the transcendent trip back to an original and perfect Eden of sorts, in itself. Time had yielded to a sweet taste of eternity.

As perhaps is fitting for such a man of intellect, Lewis describes the object of joy—God— as a chess opponent, who made moves to corner Lewis, though the final acceptance of "checkmate" was left up to Lewis to accept. A recognition of the object of joy was only the first move in a series of strategic moves; free-willed submission to God was left wholly up to Lewis, offered as a sort of presentation.

On a bus ride, a sense of self-awareness arrived in Lewis' mind as a sort of strange gift: "I became aware that I was holding something at bay, or shutting something out. Or, if you like, that I was wearing some stiff clothing, like corsets, or even a suit of armor, as if I were a lobster." Even in his imagery, Lewis' imagination was fledging along with his faith. "I felt myself being, there and then [on the bus], given a free choice. I could open the door or keep it shut; I could unbuckle the armor or keep it on…I chose to open, to unbuckle…yet it did not really seem possible to do the opposite." This wasn't exactly a moment of bliss for Lewis, who also mentions that, though he felt like "a man of snow at long last beginning to melt," he didn't particularly enjoy the sensation. Perhaps he had clung to every other philosophy for so long, his grasp was reluctant to let go, and let every aspect of himself melt into the mind to which he was acquiescing his own. "Remember, I had always wanted, above all things…to call my soul my own."

Beyond Philosophy, to Purpose

Settled into his Oxford career, and having bought a home called the Kilns, Lewis settled into a period of relative stability, sharing his household with Mrs. Moore on weekends, and living in his college rooms during the workweek. His own faith, now decided, brought however a few ripples to the unusual domestic arrangement, with Mrs. Moore quite unhappy about Lewis' new habit of getting up early on Sundays to attend church. This sort of discord Lewis also touched upon in his writings, with the claim that any household in which one member suddenly "gets" religion will see a similar upheaval.

His ambitions also writhed a bit. Though recognized as a gifted and engaging professor—and here we must recall his booming voice, knack for argument learned from Knock, and also his large physical stature—Lewis' writing career had yet to take off, and he wanted it badly. After the brief and somewhat lukewarm flash of fame which had followed the release of those poems composed during the time in the war trenches and refined in his hospital stay—poems considered mediocre at best, and whose writing he tried to keep quiet within his academic community— Lewis felt forgotten, and resented it. He had had a taste of fame, and desired greatly to be an accomplished writer. But, he complained, "I recognize myself as having unmistakably failed in it." Agitated and unsure as to how exactly being a Christian was supposed to influence his desire to write, he thought up an idea while sketching an outdoor landscape— during a visit to his father in Ireland, interestingly—and penned a prosy retelling of John Bunyan's *Pilgrim's Progress*, within the span of only two weeks, a work which Lewis titled *The Pilgrim's Regress: An allegorical apology for Christianity, Reason, and Romanticism.* Though it remains the least successful of the thirty-five volumes of prose, which he soon realized he was able to write with fluency and speed, he had finally found his genre, and ran with it from this point forward. The book, though never very popular, did serve as a starting point, as a self-created map of sorts. In *Pilgrim's Regress*, the main character John travels through similar ideological stops as Lewis himself had made along the way. In a sense, the book was a necessary map; Lewis needed to fine tune a visualization of the path he'd taken in his own mind, before he could share it with anyone else.

At this point, Lewis still had some reservations about myth itself. He still considered mythological allegories as fabricated fables— falsehoods, even—which was in opposition to the view of Tolkien, who had not at this time published anything, but had become quite engrossed with the idea of myth-*making.* Tolkien wrote and presented Lewis with a poem called *Mythopoeia* (a term coined for the creation of myth), dedicating it from "myth-lover" to "myth-hater." Through this friendship, Lewis had overcome several other things, like the taboo against "trusting a

Papist," in which Lewis transcended one of the prejudices he'd been taught as a child. Ultimately, Tolkien's legacy to Lewis, though their friendship would receive a later rift over this very issue, would be getting him to see that fiction was a vehicle through which issues of morality could be explored—though not specifically those themes of Christianity itself. Those, Tolkien believed, should be reserved only for ordained priesthood, not attempted by laypeople. Lewis, however, saw worlds of possibility opening, offering ways to bring people to a consideration of Christianity—if only obliquely, through allegory— with imagination as the carrier.

The first truly successful book Lewis wrote did not come from his own imagination; it was, funny enough, an analysis of poetry, a scholarly book titled *The Allegory of Love* which examined the ways allegory had been used in love poetry from ancient Rome through the European Renaissance. The book was, and still is, considered an incredible intellectual achievement, which altered medieval studies of English literature in particular. Ten years this work had been in the making; its success, plus the vocal support of Tolkien whose book *The Hobbit* had been a hit around this same time, gave Lewis a stronger platform with publishers for his first novel, *Out of the Silent Planet,* in 1938.

The Space Trilogy

The fictional novel of the solar system, *Out of the Silent Planet*, and its sequels which followed after a gap of years, *Perelandra* in 1943 and *That Hideous Strength* in 1945, reflect the study Lewis had put into the structure of the comprehensive biblical story, from creation and fall to redemption and renewal. The series shows how greatly Lewis had honed the moral mapmaking skill he'd first put to use in *Pilgrim's Regress*, though in the Space Trilogy, his moral explorations are laid out in ways not explicitly Christian, intentionally.

Out of the Silent Planet was written for people who, like Lewis had been in earlier days, were not religious, saw nothing but manmade mythology in the Bible, and had never attended church or had decided against ever doing so again. Openness to spirituality, not biblical creed, is promoted. Describing Earth as the only planet in the solar system that has lost its spiritual essence or "song," *Out of the Silent Planet* transports readers to other planets also in danger of infection by a similar sinister silence—in other words, planets that were in danger of falling into the clutches of evil the way Earth had, through temptation and greed. The novel was meant to serve as a precursor to the contemplation of good and evil, and particularly of consequences: Earth, or Thulcandra as it is called in the story, had clamped its ears closed to its own planetary spirit-song until it became, essentially, deaf. *Out of the Silent Planet* introduces readers to Ransom, who takes a trip to Mars, Malacandra in the story, and meets the Oyarsa of that planet. Here Lewis introduces the idea of inability to see a forest for the trees: the Oyarsa of Malacandra *is* Malacandra: its personality, its intelligence, its spirit, its uniqueness. The terrain of the planet over which the space explorers rove is simply the molecular material of which that planet is made, a feature recognizable like the face of a loved one, but only that. Every planet had an Oyarsa, but Earth, cut off from the others, was now ruled by "the Bent one."

Choices and listening, seeing beyond one's own eyes...these same themes would show up throughout Lewis' fiction in similar ways, as in *The Magician's Nephew* of the Narnia series, when the uncle, unable to hear the song of Aslan the lion singing a world into being as anything but a snarling, menacing roar, has made himself deliberately, stupidly deaf. In the Space Trilogy, the interplanetary travelers bumble around, missing the subtleties that surround them, ignorant not only of the Oyarsa but of all spiritual species, like the angelic Eldila. The underlying message is that spiritual deafness is self-perpetuating, and entirely optional.

Out of the Silent Planet commences a blurring of the margins of two disciplines in ink, planetary science, and ancient mythology.

Not only did Lewis want readers to consider good and evil and their own willingness to listen, he also begins forming a sort of synthetic body of knowledge, a blended understanding of the cosmos with every discipline in harmony. Just because the ancient Greeks and Romans assigned "personalities" to each of the planets, did that necessarily make their mythology ridiculous? If there was indeed a great mind behind every aspect of the universe which was "tingling with anthropomorphic life, a festival, not a machine" (words from Lewis' scholarly work *English Literature in the Sixteenth Century, Excluding Drama*, part of the Oxford History of English Literature and an eighteen-year onus for Lewis to write; he referred to it by acronym as his "O Hell" book) then could those ancients have had insight into the spiritual presence living throughout? After all, Earth itself, like the human mind, was so much more than molecules and mechanics.

But Lewis adds a footnote to readers who think they see what he's up to if they recognize the overarching biblical theme of redemption of a world, in the preface of the second novel of the trilogy, *Perelandra*: "All the human characters in this book are purely fictitious and none of them is allegorical." As humans have to this day still not set foot on other planets, this seems a silly way of pointing out the obvious, but Lewis included it to dispel the idea that his books could be used as a sort of alternate retelling of those stories of—and only of— the Bible.

Good and Evil, and World War II

The latter two installments of the Space Trilogy, *Perelandra* and *That Hideous Strength*, were constructed during World War II and the many other engagements Lewis was involved with during the war period, including other works of fiction, and non-fiction which dealt more explicitly with the real and pertinent questions of faith. Along with never wearing a watch and leaving his Oxford lecture attendees hanging with provocative, unanswerable questions, Lewis was known for doing two things at once, often penning two vastly differing bodies of work at the same time, alternating between them as a sort of refreshment for his mind.

The year 1940 saw the publication of *The Problem of Pain*, which argued for the existence of God in the midst of turmoil and suffering. This, naturally, was of tremendous interest to Britain in the midst of yet another war, as many people had some forthright questions for God: Why did He allow suffering? Why would an all-powerful being allow war to happen at all? Did prayer ever really make a difference?

Lewis lent his own experience to these valid grievances, the very same questions with which he himself had wrestled. His dealings with them were so well-received that in 1941, he was summoned to go beyond the written word. Lewis was asked by the BBC to deliver a series of addresses over radio, a series of live talks on Wednesday evenings of fifteen minutes each, in which he read his own work. At Lewis' insistence, an additional fifth episode was added, during which he would answer questions mailed in by listeners. This addition is notable in that it shows just how strongly Lewis felt it his duty to respond personally, a trait which would characterize Lewis' dealings in future years with correspondence he received from listeners and readers. (Though much of the mail he received was filled with questions about his books, or guesses as to what the elements in his fiction represented, Lewis also received stacks of requests for counseling, personal assistance, money, and prayer. To most of these he faithfully and dutifully replied, often spending two to three hours a day penning letters back. As with many who find fame, Lewis had a few correspondents who became rather obsessive in their admiration; a couple of women insisted they were in love with or even engaged to Lewis. One of these went so far as to take out a line of credit at a swanky hotel as "Mrs. Lewis," and, when caught in the lie, was sent to prison. Claiming she was dying, the woman wrote begging Lewis—who didn't drive— to visit her, and astonishingly, probably out of pity for the hale and hearty deluded woman, he did.) Collectively, the collected transcripts of this broadcast series is titled *Right and Wrong*.

That same year, 1941, a series of thirty-one weekly installments of a heaven-and-hell story was run in The Guardian (a now-defunct religious newspaper not to be confused with the Manchester Guardian), a series with so original and odd an angle of examining good and evil that the printed collection of installments continues to be one of Lewis' best-known works of fiction for adults. Titled *The Screwtape Letters*, the story consists of a series of letters written by a high-ranking executive officer of the devil himself, and is a highly amusing satire of the trials of human life. Screwtape, an agent of evil working for "Our Father Below," coaches his entry-level nephew—a demon—as the younger pursues the damnation of a young human fellow. "My dear Wormwood," the uncle begins each week's correspondence, often following the greeting with a chastisement of the nephew's blunders, plus some coaching advice as to how to exploit the insecurities and temptations of humans. "Everything has to be *twisted* before it is any use to us." The enemy's (God's) methods are put to every possible corruption, tempting the human through sickness and health. Readers of the series saw their own foibles mirrored in the choices, health, and romantic life of the pursued subject, a creature referred to by Uncle Screwtape as just another of a species of "vermin so muddled in mind."

Lewis admits that though this "device of diabolical letters" came easily to him as a writer, the series wasn't one he particularly enjoyed making. "The world into which I had to project myself while I spoke through Screwtape was all dust, grit, thirst, and itch...It almost smothered me before I was done." He felt there ought to have been a proper counterpoint for the Father Above, such as an angel, offering guidance to counterbalance the onslaught of temptation slung at the poor human. But Lewis didn't feel that he—or anyone, as a corruptible human—could ever produce such a venerable viewpoint, and gave all proceeds from *The Screwtape Letters*, along with much of his other writings' earnings, to charity.

The Great Divorce

After the war, Lewis put forth another fantasy novel about heaven, hell, and the impact of free will. Interestingly, as his own moment of coming to faith via free will came (by his recollection in *Surprised by Joy*) on a bus, the novel is set on a tour bus that travels through the disparate realms of heaven and hell. The two places, Lewis insists, could never coexist. Evil was evil, and could never be altered, and one could never keep even a small "souvenir" of hell and expect to see heaven. Only by backpedaling and returning to the path of good could one shirk evil and be rid of it. This, of course, involved full confrontation with one's own flaws. The two eternities were mutually exclusive, a very different notion from the marriage of them as written by Blake. Humbly acknowledging Blake's literature classic and how the story inspired his own novel's name, *The Great Divorce*, Lewis proffers his counterpoint. "Blake wrote the Marriage of Heaven and Hell. If I have written of their Divorce, this is not because I think myself a fit antagonist for so great a genius, nor even because I feel at all sure that I know what he meant. (*The Great Divorce,* preface.)" Lewis sees the two places as distinct destinations: "It is still 'either-or.'" Not even time could take evil and reinvent it.

Before he boards the reader as tourist passenger on the expedition of *The Great Divorce*, Lewis issues two interesting things in its preface: First, a nod of thanks to an unknown (to him) American author of science fiction, whose piece in a magazine inspired Lewis; the other, a direct warning against taking any of the heaven and hell tour as fact: "I beg readers to remember that this is a fantasy. It has of course—or I intended it to have—a moral. But the transmortal conditions are solely an imaginative supposal: they are not even a guess or a speculation what may actually await us. The last thing I wish is to arouse factual curiosity about the details of the after-world." Coming from the man who had clung onto desire for self-governance for so long, this reveals how much Lewis had grown into acceptance of imagination as a trustworthy compass. The heaven of which he wrote was beyond the capacity of facts to ever explain. Imagination was the only way to know what was beyond the measurability of the senses, and of science.

With the tour underway, everyday choices are made suspect. And all have consequences. Readers meet supernatural beings, some of whom have chosen hell indirectly by wrapping themselves in its grasp and refusing to die to their former, living selves, and in so doing accept the fullness of new life and rebirth offered by heaven. The ghosts become mere crumbs of their former selves, fading desperately away while still clinging to the reins, to the false gods of self and material life.

False gods were another theme Lewis gave much consideration, in that they can take so many forms. A determinedly old-fashioned man who refused to learn to use a typewriter and wrote everything by hand, Lewis was suspicious even of progress itself. He had seen the faults in mistaking what is modern for what is true, and of pursuing progress only for progress' sake. The cycle consumed those caught up in it, and truth could be so easily lost sight of, when this was the case. Too much confidence in progress or any other false god caused one to give away a part of one's own truth, and shrink away, withering into a ghost like one of those lost drifting spirits of *The Great Divorce*, or, like John of *The Pilgrim's Regress,* failing to see the immediacy of one's own homestead as a part of something much larger. One had to step away from one's own era, or perspective, or upbringing, or Christian denomination, far enough to see it as part of a whole, a much larger picture. Sticking stubbornly to anything—even a political party or school of philosophy—was creating a false god for oneself, and put one at risk of damnation.

At the conclusion of *The Great Divorce* tour Lewis lets the reader off with further directions to continue onward. He refers the reader to a particular translation of the New Testament, with a warning that further study might lead a student of the Bible to feel like a sheep among wolves. The opinions and writings of many biblical examiners, even clergymen, often retained that default, ingrained by modernism's rationalist view of miracles as impossibilities. Naturalism was so much simpler and more palatable, with its God who played by nature's rules. Releasing one's comfortable views required serious effort.

Perhaps it was recognition of this complicated leap of faith—his own "bridge" across the chasm that had been built with exhaustive intellectual effort—that led Lewis to write children's fiction that wasn't necessarily for just children.

Miracles

"Seeing is not believing," states *Miracles* at the start. "For this reason, the question whether miracles occur can never be answered simply by experience." Evidence, again, is shown to be not wide enough a lens to perceive truth, at least not by itself. Published in 1947, this volume of apologetics and logic may offer the clearest insight into both Lewis' mind and journey from non-belief to faith of all, and issues an invitation of sorts to the reader—outright, this time— to join the author in a sort of readable flow chart of decision-making, with Lewis serving as a mixture of ally and devil's advocate. Not only are the personal revelations in *Miracles* some of the frankest of his own Christian journey, the path that they outline are presented in a manner that seems almost contrary to Lewis' stated dislike of walking and talking at the same time, as he escorts the reader through each step of logic, arriving at the almost inescapable conclusion, that of belief.

By the time he penned *Miracles,* Lewis had grown quite comfortable with the existence of two things in one. This shows up in the way he presents the debate between the opposing views of nature, or the idea that the universe is an all-encompassing closed circuit, with nothing external to it, and Supernature, meaning nature plus something beyond which can be neither measured nor perceived. (Readers should note that, by his use of the word "Supernature," Lewis did not mean a world full of ghosts and inexplicable occurrences. He invented the term— or at least a definition of it, to use in this particular work— feeling that it would encompass the whole "something more than nature" viewpoint of the common reader, and was an acceptable term to use for popular literature. By this time Lewis was well-aware that he had become a popular, layperson apologist for Christianity, and was using this status to further the cause as he saw fit.) A narrowing comparison, in a sort of elimination round of philosophy, examines the possibilities offered by either viewpoint, and stretches throughout the entire course of the book.

In *Miracles,* Lewis does not offer justification for inexplicable events. Rather, he claims that any and all of those occurrences we would commonly call "miracles" (rare events, in his opinion), all relate back to the only one that matters: the Incarnation. This is the single miracle upon which everything else that ever has or ever will happen depends. Miracles of healing, transformation, virgin birth, or anything else are not considered, only that single intersection of the God of Supernature deliberately collapsing Himself into Nature, condescending to descend and rise again and bring the whole world back up with Him. And all of nature reflects this one divine event: "The pattern is there in Nature because it was first there in God. All the instances...turn out to be but transpositions of the Divine theme into a minor key."

"Christ's death and rebirth are a perfect fit—they *design* the fit—of the entire Creation. I am not now referring simply to the Crucifixion and Resurrection of Christ. The total pattern, of which they are only the turning point, is the real death and rebirth: for certainly no seed ever fell from so fair a tree into so dark and cold a soil as...in which God dredged the salt and oozy bottom of Creation." Everything was one, heaven and Earth intersecting in this one point in time. And all of the smaller things ever witnessed were simply echoes of that original descent and reascent.

True to form, Lewis first shows his reader the wide, wide lens, this time the whole world and everything in it. Then come choices, offered like a vascular system narrowing from arteries into capillaries. Shall we see nature as a closed package deal, with explanations for everything including our highly-evolved brains' creation of the notion of a God, or shall we view it as a realm with something larger behind it providing the mind for all our own reflections of mind?

With argument after argument, the choices narrow down by elimination, Lewis never telling the reader what to think, only inviting him *to* think, and to think hard, mirroring the style of "Old Knock" Kirkpatrick and pointing out the holes in each argument as well as the perils of clinging to any philosophy that chases its own tail. What makes *Miracles* unique is that, in it, Lewis begins to point out the holes in his *own* choices—the pitfalls that strike anyone who has begun to walk along the same path he himself has trod. Firmly settled in Christian belief—and indeed, an authority upon it—by this time in his life, Lewis notes every exit strategy along the thinking person's path, and gives anyone following in his footsteps some answers. The author becomes an encourager, his writing still walking and talking readers along the journey to faith.

For someone who insisted in his biography that science was never his thing— that the "lion of Mathematics" was too hard an obstacle to overcome and pursue further study— Lewis reveals a deep understanding of the physical sciences in this book. So deep is this grasp that he uses examples from the nature of subatomic particle behavior, neuroscience, astronomy, and evolution—all pure sciences that study nature as nature, and by their own "nature" do not seek the whys but only the whats and hows— as bolsters to the viewpoint that nature is tied to the supernatural.

Never does Lewis see science as a threat to belief in God; quite the contrary. What he does view as a tremendous threat is the movement away from poetry and folktale. His comments here on the book of Genesis show just how much Lewis has come to value that creative half of the mind, which reflects that of the Creator Himself: "We are inveterate poets…Our imaginations awake." In regards to the great power of the mind, not all human minds were capable of probing the great mysteries of it equally, he says, nor of the sciences whose mathematics were beautiful and complicated. Poetic stories—with the Hebrew story of Genesis being the only one not to run in circles—were the most accessible way to enter into these mysteries. That is, at least, until the Age of Enlightenment, when rationalism was born and scientific scrutiny took over. There was great danger to be found in the modern era. "All over the world, until quite modern times, the direct insight of mystics and the reasonings of the philosophers percolated to the mass of the people by authority and tradition; they could be received by those who were no great reasoners themselves in the concrete form of myth and ritual and the whole pattern of life. In the conditions produced by a century or so of Naturalism, plain men are being forced to bear burdens which plain men were never expected to bear before." Though it sounds a tad like intellectual snobbery, Lewis was simply arguing that allegories like the Creation story are gifts of poetry, which keep open the portals to God for everyone. Allegory could be a joyful song, a vehicle that accommodated all those drawn to something beyond, no matter what nimbleness of mind they had been granted. Imagination made sure no one drawn to God was left out.

Lewis also says that there are dire consequences for a world in which the masses (the majority of people) are still as "simple" as they have always been, historically, but in which the Supernaturalist seers— the poetic mythmakers—are no longer listened to. "[Those societies] can achieve only superficiality, baseness, ugliness, and in the end extinction." When leaders no longer listen for the song, whole nations grow deaf to God.

Full Admittance

Having presented both the "only nature exists" and "there's something more, and that something is a God who isn't standoffish, but could come after us if He chose to" sides of the argument, Lewis admits in *Miracles*, and would later elaborate in *Surprised by Joy*, that the biggest hurdle he ever faced on the route to a fully alive faith was an unpleasant admittance that God was an untamable, living entity: "It is always shocking to meet life where we thought we were alone. 'Look out!' we cry, 'it is *alive*'."

Lewis describes feeling that God was a chess player, of sorts. One had to be ready, for He might come after you. In *Miracles*, he likens this to a group of children who have been pretending they heard robbers. "There comes a moment when the children who have been playing at burglars hush suddenly: was that a *real* footstep in the hall? There comes a moment when people who have been dabbling in religion ('Man's search for God!') suddenly draw back. Supposing we really found Him? We never meant it to come to *that*! Worse still, supposing He had found us?" What a strange analogy: God as an assailant?

The analogy is an uncomfortable one, similar to when Lewis described the moment that forced the issues of free will and surrender, which closed in upon Lewis on that particular bus ride when he "gave in" and accepted God; recall his rather claustrophobia-inducing description of that bus ride: "[I felt] that I was wearing some stiff clothing, like corsets, or even a suit of armor, as if I were a lobster." Lewis may be trying to tell the reader that the road of Christian faith is not necessarily an easy one, and that, like that "lobster" in a tight shell, there will be setbacks and multiple occasions to grow along the way. He bluntly exhorts anyone choosing the Christian path to be forewarned: "You must not do, you must not even try to do, the will of the Father unless you are prepared to 'know of the doctrine.'" In other words, when giving in to God's will, it is going to be all—an uncomfortable all— or nothing. At least he's honest about it. Lewis freely acknowledges that his own willful nature never gave in easily. Killing the self may be quite a bit more than a one-time occasion, but "the deeper the death the brighter the rebirth," he writes in *Miracles*, also pointing out that "Men are reluctant to pass over from the notion of an abstract and negative deity to the living God. I do not wonder...The Pantheist's God does nothing, demands nothing. He is there if you wish for Him, like a book on a shelf. He will not pursue you. There is no danger that at any time heaven and earth should flee away at his glance."

He goes on to say that bumpiness is a standard feature in the journey of God's people, illustrating the trials and sufferings of the Hebrews. Abraham suffered an ordeal; Mary, an ordeal of the heart. With each of God's chosen people, there was a mirrored experience of that great shrinking act God performed in demeaning Himself to come to Earth, suffer, and rise, through the Man of Sorrows who sank to the very bottoms of the horrors that existed on Earth, and rose again "disabling Death itself (*Mere Christianity*)." Lewis sympathizes with anyone reading along that constant sacrifice was impossibly hard, and only total surrender, in form of death to the self, could make it happen. Killing of the "self" was the only way to cast off an unfulfilled life and have it replaced by the new; rebirth was not possible otherwise. It wouldn't be an accurate reflection of what God had done.

Nor was it possible to attain this fullness singlehandedly: "Nothing in nature can ever exist alone, independent of anything else: everything that lives does so because it eats, breathes, and gets what it needs from external sources. The minute it tries to detach, it dies." The slightly terrifying acceptance of God as God's own self, outside any of our own controls upon Him, is hardly comforting. But then, nothing God did when intersecting with nature—that one great miracle—ever was. Nor was it a cushy ride for any of the people God ever chose, from the Hebrew people to the prophets to the unwed pregnant teen who bore the Christ Child. "You have noticed, I expect," Lewis offers in *Mere Christianity*, "that Christ Himself sometimes describes the Christian way as very hard, sometimes as very easy. He says 'Take up your Cross'—in other words, it is like going to be beaten to death in a concentration camp. Next minute he says, 'My yoke is easy and my burden light.' He means both." Always Lewis was aware of the presence of duality, of two things at the same time, both true.

Mere Christianity

The work now published as *Mere Christianity* is also a compilation of Lewis' radio addresses, delivered from 1942 to 1944 as World War II held Britain under the constant anxiety of air raids and the strictures of rationing. Once so fond of pleasant solitude among books and of self-directed days, Lewis at this time was owned by a frenzied daily schedule filled with dutiful engagement to readers, listeners, and, of course, university students. Lewis was asked, again, to give a series of talks, and this he did, the talks guiding listeners along much the same course of logic as had the chapters in *Miracles*, with Lewis revealing his thought processes drop by drop, always starting with a wide view of "everything" and paring down the scope. Adapting his style of language to better suit a popular—and war-weary—radio audience, Lewis gave this series of talks, offering much the same course of apologetic reasoning as he did in *Miracles*, but without the esoteric language he usually used in the university setting. These talks addressed some of Lewis' big-picture views on faith, namely the traps of self, with some advice on practical matters, and of denominational disagreements.

Like in *Miracles*, Lewis reminded radio listeners about the dangers of stubborn self-subsistence. An individual trying stubbornly to retain a relationship with God based on his own terms would be failing to confront just how flawed and incapable he really was, thus turning confession into a farce. Only in full surrender could one truly let God in, and that meant giving up control and one's own parameters of what God was and wasn't. Some weekly episodes addressed the virtues, behaviors, and applied moralities of Christianity, including a highly controversial chapter on marriage for which he is often criticized. (Lewis was, at the time of these radio talks, yet unmarried; not only was he personally unqualified to write about the subject, he also offers argument justifying the subservience of wife to husband—a volatile and divisive subject, then and now.) Listeners were encouraged not only to submit themselves fully over to God, but to practice, daily, the applications of faith: "...God designed the human machine to run on Himself. He Himself is the fuel our spirits were designed to burn, or the food our spirits were designed to feed on. There is no other. That is why it is just no good asking God to make us happy in our own way without bothering about religion. God cannot give us a happiness and peace apart from Himself, because it is not there. There is no such thing." And there was no getting around those rules of individual governance which the faith provided; those rules were there for a reason, Lewis insists.

As for the arguments between Christian denominations, over such ideologies like whether it was good works or faith alone which leads to heaven, not only did Lewis feel it was ridiculous to be arguing over particulars, it was an erosive waste of time. "The central Christian belief is that Christ's death has somehow put us right with God and given us a fresh start. Theories as to how it did this are another matter." The essence of the redeeming gift was lost, if one got caught up in the *how,* and became preoccupied with it. All that matters is *why* God sent His son. That was the essence not to be lost.

The series also pointed out the absurdities of faith, particularly the notion that nothing, when it comes to God's doings, is ever predictable. Nothing is regular, not even the orbits of the planets themselves, for example, which as humans we tend to want to simplify into perfect circles. That, Lewis warns, would be too easy. God, and the ways through which He revealed Himself, were arbitrary and quirky, never predictable, and this capriciousness was reflected throughout the entire universe.

Faith, Lewis said, was an audacity in itself; accepting what could only be explained by admitting that there *was* something inexplicable was daring to the point of lunacy. And yet, "[all] I am doing is asking people to face the facts," he claims, arguing that there are only two views that can encompass these facts, if one has accepted the presence of an organization mind at work in the world: Full acceptance of the God incarnate in Christ, or dualism, the belief that there were two separate powers "at the back of everything." But one of them, dualism, has a flaw: At any stage of its argument, there comes a point at which there must exist something *more*, some value by which the idea of justice or basic universal right and wrong always brushes up against. No matter how far back the argument tries to reduce the Universe, dualism always hits that moral wall and ceases to explain anything further.

If one has gone with God as that great mind, then practice—in the same way as a child plays with dress-up clothing, playing at being an adult—was the only way to help oneself grow into the spiritual garments of faith; eventually the mature mind would come to the "practical conclusion" that Jesus was, indeed, who he said he was. Along these lines, it is in *Mere Christianity* that Lewis offers the most barefaced choice of all: Either a person can accept that Jesus Christ is who he says he is, or concede to saying he was a megalomaniac. No middle ground exists, no soft argument claiming Jesus as a great moral teacher. "I am trying here to prevent anyone saying the really foolish thing that people often say about Him: 'I'm ready to accept Jesus as a great moral teacher, but I don't accept His claim to be God.' That is the one thing we must not say. A man who was merely a man and said the sort of things Jesus said would not be a great moral teacher. He would either be a lunatic-on a level with the man who says he is a poached egg-or else he would be the Devil of

Hell. You must make your choice. Either this man was, and is, the Son of God: or else a madman or something worse. You can shut him up for a fool, you can spit at Him and kill Him as a demon; or you can fall at His feet and call Him Lord and God." The choice could not be outlined any more severely; the power of this address with Lewis' own powerful intonation must have caused quite a sensation over the radio waves.

The popular audience listening to these installments were also given some insight as to why God tied His divine to some very concrete, ordinary things of everyday life, from the water of baptism, to the act of eating in Holy Communion. Again, all was tied to God's condescending to send Himself through a bottleneck of sorts and become mundane, that he might rise up again and elevate the world with Him. "God …invented eating. He likes matter. He invented it." And "[Lewis] cannot see for [himself] why these things should be the conductors of new life…[but] the whole mass of Christians are the physical organism through which Christ acts…we are His fingers and muscles, the cells of His body. And perhaps that explains why this new life is spread not only by purely mental acts like belief, but by bodily acts like baptism and Holy Communion…God never meant man to be a purely spiritual creature. That is why He uses material things like bread and wine to put the new life into us."

Lewis even adopts the lowliest, earthiest imagery thinkable to represent Christian fellowship: Germs. The Christian God, he claims, is the only one among religions who has never been presented as a static thing, but as one living and dynamic—a "good" infection, which spreads. "One of our own race (Jesus) has this new life: if we get close to Him we shall catch it from him (*Mere Christianity*)." And as this new life comes by way of the extended hands of fellowship, Lewis expresses his gratitude to the many hands which were extended to him throughout his life—not all in invitation to the Christian faith, but as helpful tugs along his personal journey: "Men are mirrors, or 'carriers' of Christ to other men. Sometimes unconscious carriers. This 'good infection' can be carried by those who have not got it themselves. People who were not Christians themselves helped me to Christianity...That is why the Church, the whole body of Christians showing Him to one another, is so important."

Narnia

Gratitude itself is a good place to begin looking at the many things Lewis incorporated into his beloved epic of fantasy, the Narnian chronicles, in that he there acknowledges the many influences from not only his childhood years, but those valued in his life at the time the first of the series of novels was written, by naming characters after them. Released in 1950 when the author was fifty-two years old, *The Lion, The Witch, and The Wardrobe* commenced what would become a seven book series, with one volume added per subsequent year, though Lewis did not set out with the idea of writing a complete series when he started out. The stories came to him as he went along.

For a man who listed his favorite sound as "adult male laughter," it seems odd that Lewis chose to write—and is so well remembered for—works for children. But imagination, as the illuminating principle of God, had by this time of Lewis' life reached full flow, and his pen and publishers could hardly keep up. Writing for and about the people and beliefs he held dear, Lewis recaps so much of his life experience in the Narnia series that the story almost pours out like gratitude for the joys—and trials — of the faith journey itself.

By the time Narnia was introduced to readers, Lewis was able to look back over his life and see the great number of flaws that made him quite human, flaws he was able, finally if obliquely, to let out of his heart and share. He had passed from happy childhood through grief, on to miserable school experiences that would today be called bullying, to the "delightfully selfish" (and sometimes snotty and arrogant, in his letters home) academic studies and successes of his teen years, on to the horrors and nightmares of war, the demands of a professional career he disliked, and the tumultuous, demanding relationship with Mrs. Moore. In Narnia, Lewis doesn't "animate" the way he did in his childhood Animal Land drawings, always remaining apart from them as puppeteer; rather, he turns himself inside out, yielding wholeheartedly to the revelatory power of divine imagination and imbuing the stories with his own self. In that sense, Narnia is "begat," mirroring the way God begat Creation; perhaps that honest reflection contributes to the stories' continued popularity.

Readers of *The Lion, The Witch, and The Wardrobe* were introduced to a quartet of children: Lucy, Edmund, Peter, and Susan; as well as a Professor Kirke, whose drafty old house was as important a story character to Lewis as the humans who roamed it and discovered the magic portal found at the back of one of its wardrobes. Lucy, youngest of the fictional siblings, was also the name of one of Lewis' godchildren, the daughter of his good friend Owen Barfield. Presumably, Lewis wrote to entertain her, and saw the opportunity presented in so doing. He could do for children what he had already done successfully for adults, and open minds to the possibility of the symbiosis of fact and fable. Imagination and reason did not have to be at odds; if young readers could be trained early enough to keep that possibility alive (Lewis abhorred the way university students often arrived with their minds already closed, which he blamed on the way teachers imbued growing minds with skepticism, and the way they tried to strip away any value judgements in language itself), then might their experiences in life be less characterized by that constant internal battle of discerning truth from fiction?

In keeping visible that frontier of the mind—that place where reason and imagination intersect—Lewis shows a pretty good understanding of how children's minds work, and of how they perceive the world. Readers step right into the Narnian story not from the perspective of an adult, but from that of other children, forming as the characters do their first impressions of the hidden wonders in the land at the back of the wardrobe. And the character children's decisions are just as easy to place oneself into and rationalize as Lewis' apologetic arguments for adults.

Lucy, youngest of the siblings, stumbles into Narnia before any of her siblings do, meeting and accepting the faun Tumnus without judgment. She returns to the old house where the four are staying as war seizes Britain, exclaiming over her adventures to skeptical siblings who either jeer at her as Edmund does, wanting to hide his own subsequent foray into Narnia, or express concern at her sanity. Adult readers can reasonably assume that Lewis put a bit of his own initial response to Christian beliefs—that of incredulity— into the reception young Lucy receives. Such a story was simply absurd.

He certainly put much of himself into the character of Edmund, or at least the self Lewis was when he was Edmund's age, miserable at school and stuck in the shadow of an older brother. Edmund all too readily allies himself with the White Witch whom he meets at his own first foray into Narnia. The witch knowing how to bait him and use his weaknesses to her advantage, just like Screwtape the uncle did, in his letters to his nephew; offering to make Edmund a Prince—and someday, King, and if he returns with the rest of his siblings, the witch says she'll also make Peter a subservient Duke. This delightful prospect, the warmth of drink, and sweet addiction of the Witch's enchanted Turkish delight all sink their seemingly harmless claws into Edmund, and ultimately create his need for redemption. Lewis wrote to show children that there is a bit of Edmund in everyone, as well as bits of Susan and Peter, and sweet Lucy, too: innocence and awe, criticism and rejection, desire, character flaws, and honor. All are part of the human mix.

One can also assume that the personality of Professor Kirke, named to echo Lewis' old mentor Kirkpatrick (and possibly the Scottish word for the church, "Kirk") was acknowledgement of that tutor so full of eccentricity, sharp expressions, and surprises—and, as always, vigorous insistence on logic. In *The Lion, The Witch, and The Wardrobe*, though, that logic spins off on a separate "what if" course than the atheism of the real-life teacher. Kirke's mannerisms may be quite similar to Old Knock, at least in the way the "very old man with shaggy white hair" responds to elder siblings Peter and Susan when they relay their little sister's queer tale of a snowy realm at the back of a piece of furniture. But where Kirk ended up at atheism, Kirke lands in (at least as far as the reader learns in this first novel) Agnosticism. Lewis has taken alternate reality for a spin.

"'How do you know...that your sister's story is not true?'" Kirke asks. And "anyone could see from the old man's face that he was perfectly serious." A logical debate with Peter and Susan follows, one in which the brother and sister are shown to believe that which has always proven to be more truthful— in this case, Lucy. "You know she doesn't tell lies and unless any further evidence turns up, we must assume that she is telling the truth." Susan, barely acquainted with the man who is housing them safely in the English countryside, "never dreamed that a grownup would talk like the Professor and didn't know what to think."

Professor Kirke claims to know very little about the house he inhabits, a house Lucy feels "far larger…than she had ever been in before" and which "made her feel a little creepy." It was "the sort of house that you never seem to come to the end of." Many curious parties of adults applied to the housekeeper for a tour of the vast place, and it is one of these events, abhorred by the children, that chases the siblings into another round with the enchanted closet, Lewis recreating the unease he felt about God early on as well as that sense of being "chased" into faith.

All four children, whether "it was that they lost their heads, or that Mrs Macready [the housekeeper] was trying to catch them, or that some magic in the house had come to life and was chasing them into Narnia," were brought together in the new world: the doubters, the cheerful insisters, and the agnostics all together. This diversity displays another feature of Lewis' understanding of a healthy body of Christianity: That in heterogeneity, there is reflection of God. At the end of the series, at which the old worlds end and a New Narnia is ushered in, the wide spectrum of creatures from all worlds come together into "the land [they] have been looking for all [their] life," a world that is both familiar and unlike anything of the world they once knew.

Time and Place and Truth

Other writers and critics have both disdained and praised Lewis for what they consider Biblical allegory in the Narnia books, the critics claiming Lewis had ulterior motives and used the series as a means of planting seeds of Christianity into the minds of unsuspecting children, the others attempting to sleuth out the direct Biblical parallels. Lewis refutes both these claims.

Along with the rest of his non-scholarly work, Lewis considers his own writing to be evangelical, but says that Narnia was not written as another Christian apologetic exercise. The overarching themes of redemption, surrogate sacrifice, evil and good are all present in the Narnian epic, but they're presented intentionally distinct from those themes as encountered in the Bible—present as a series of "what ifs," as already seen in the twist given to Professor Kirke. Such "what ifs" wondered how redemption by God might have taken place in other places in Creation. In a letter written in response to one young reader of the series, Lewis explains: "...I'm not exactly "representing" the real (Christian) story in symbols. I'm more saying "Suppose there were a world like Narnia and it needed rescuing and the Son of God (or the 'Great Emperor oversea') went to redeem *it*, as He came to redeem ours, what might it, in that world, all have been like?"

All of Narnia, from story content to literary device, points back to Lewis' fascination with time and space, and all that lies outside of what we here on Earth experience. Children both real and fictitious are invited to examine their own worlds and wrestle with what they believe to be real, to stay open to more than what their eyes and ears tell them, and always seek truth. Lucy, when she tumbles back out of the wardrobe the first time and re-enters the Professor's house, insists that she has been absent for hours, yet only a few "house" minutes have passed— no longer than a game of hide-and-seek. This is what prompts her older brother and sister to question her sanity, but Peter and Susan are invited to seek truth where evidence speaks to the contrary.

In modern physics, there is much investigation into the flexibility of space and time and how they bend to accommodate the unchanging speed of light, principles with which Lewis was familiar despite that "lion" of mathematical computations and algebra, which kept him from studying the sciences academically. The idea that time was not a static quantity, that minutes on Earth might be milliseconds or eons elsewhere, was an irresistible inspiration: What would it be like, if there were a portal between Earth and some other world? How would time as we know and experience it here be shown to have little or no meaning? Echoes of that "chronological snobbery" issue that Lewis discarded (with help from Barfield and Tolkien) show up in the way Lewis moved back and forth in Earth time, penning prequels and sequels out of order when writing the Narnia series itself.

Time, and age as we know it on this planet, are of little importance; there is an eternal self that isn't stuck in the timeline of a lifetime. As for space, Lewis' inhabitants of other worlds were given freedom of choice, just like humans: Should an apple with magical healing properties be eaten selfishly, or carried dutifully back to where it belonged, as instructed by Aslan? Lewis contemplated these what-ifs in *The Magician's Nephew*, exploring the choices he himself would have made if he had been offered in childhood an apple that could have restored his mother's health and prevented her death.

Just as the choice of an animal savior in Aslan was simplified— Lewis felt children would more readily identify with a suffering animal than a human adult historical figure who lived thousands of years before they did—so were the concrete symbols of Aslan's sacrifice, meant to suggest but not mirror the elements of Christian liturgy: The stone table upon which Aslan is sacrificed cracks into two, a sound and visual easily conjured, which rolls together the table of the Last Supper and the loaf of bread broken there, and also the table of Moses and the tombstone rolled away at Jesus' grave. Lewis also keeps Narnian battle scenes softened, blurry in some cases, and boundaries between good and evil firmer, devices also adapted for the sake of child readers. Only in his works written for adults did Lewis go at length into complicated analysis of coexistence of good and evil in one free-willed mind—or on a larger scale, one whole planet—though the idea is introduced in the interactions of the siblings. Playing with the idea of two concrete worlds was enough for concrete-thinking children, enough to inspire their own imaginations to reunite what seemed like disparate entities.

The one great miracle of Narnia, the root from which all else grows just as God's incarnation on Earth creates every smaller miracle, is considered by many the strongest case for direct allegory. The sacrifice and humiliation of Aslan the lion, with all the accompanying jeering and mane-shaving and taunts he receives, do deliberately echo that shrinking condescension and arisen life of Jesus Christ, but Narnia's miracle is meant to be kept separate from the sacrifice of Christ—it is not the same thing. The Narnian miracle does restore Edmund, the stone creatures, and the whole Land of Narnia, breaking the spell of winter, but mainly it resurrects the wonder of imagination: That land in which children are born and over which they deserve to not only enter but reign, as do Peter, Susan, Edmund, and Lucy equally as kings and queens at the end of *The Lion, The Witch, and The Wardrobe.* The harsh, inhospitable, endless winter of human lives guided by reason alone have been redeemed, in a smaller but significant way, by a lion.

Last Battle

As we have noted, Lewis recognized and wrote that the Christian journey was never meant to be an easy one. And in the last years of his life, he experienced a mixed swirl of that joy he had always sought, along with plenty of frustration, grief, disappointment, and sorrow.

Numerous people who wrote to Lewis eventually became regular correspondents, even faraway friends. One of these, a married American poet and novelist who was mother of two boys, and who had converted from Judaism to Christianity, wrote with a sharpness of wit that captured Lewis' interest. Joy Davidman Gresham, a tiny woman with loudly uninhibited personality, was stuck in a crumbling marriage, and in 1953, only a few years after the death of Mrs. Moore (which provided a fresh start for Lewis), moved to England with her young sons in tow. She was only thirty-nine years old; Lewis was fifty-five.

As Mrs. Moore's life waned, Lewis himself became somewhat preoccupied with the process of growing old, and of loss of vitality. His career had had disappointments, in that Oxford never promoted Lewis to a full professorial chair, which would have relieved him of the time commitments of being a lesser-ranked tutor. Even though his scholarly publications had been well received, certain members of the university viewed Lewis' outside writings as a waste of time and talent in genres that were certainly not academic.

Lewis had waited years for promotion, as others, including his friend Tolkien, had been appointed to full professorship. Interestingly, Tolkien went to bat for Lewis when a promotion was finally offered. Cambridge University offered Lewis a position in Medieval and Renaissance Literature, but Lewis turned it down, feeling both that he was too old and that he could not move away from his brother Warnie, whose alcoholism was worsening. Though the two were not on close terms at the time, Tolkien had seen a great success with *The Lord of the Rings* and had not forgotten the encouragement Lewis had given him in creating it, and urged both Lewis and the department, who had offered the post to someone else, to reconsider. Lewis and the University accepted, and Lewis decided to commute. Oxford hastily put together a counteroffer, which Lewis refused.

With much more time free after the change of job and ending of his thirty-year commitment to Mrs. Moore, Lewis enjoyed something of a release, and was able to enjoy himself—and, often, the company of Joy Gresham. Though Lewis was either unaware of or in denial of the developing relationship, others saw it. Warnie saw Joy to be pursuing Lewis determinedly, even before her divorce was final. She and her sons came to the Lewis' brothers' home at The Kilns for the holidays, then increasingly often, until Joy moved within walking distance. Her own finances were meager; Lewis, who by this time was financially stable, paid for both her boys' schooling. Though Lewis clearly enjoyed her company, the relationship might not have changed but for two events: Joy's threat of deportation back to the United States, and a broken bone.

Claiming the civil marriage to be nothing more than an act of "friendship" on his part, Lewis agreed to marry Joy Gresham, assuring others that nothing would change except Joy's ability to remain in England. Lewis claimed he had no romantic attachment to her whatsoever, something his brother disagreed with; in Warnie's diary, he wrote that he viewed the whole thing as part of a strategic plan of pursuit by Joy. As Joy still had little money, plans were made to relocate her to The Kilns. Then came the phone call that changed things. Standing to answer a call, Joy tripped and her femur snapped. Doctors discovered that cancer had eaten most of the bone away, and a long course of surgical treatments followed.

Periods of intense joy and sorrow began, often in concurrent mixed blessing: Joy entered a period of what was thought to be full recovery, but Lewis' own skeleton was collapsing with osteoporosis. The Cambridge environment suited him well and the University was delighted to have him, and Lewis was asked to do yet another series of radio talks, this time to an American audience, examining the many forms of love. (These became in print *The Four Loves*.) Lewis and his wife were able to enjoy travels abroad, until the day she received news that her cancer was back, and had metastasized throughout her skeleton. A trip to Greece was embarked upon anyway; Joy died only a few weeks afterwards.

Lewis, was, in a sense very like his own mother. Flora had been a woman of high intellect but little expressed emotion, and even to Lewis' father Arthur she never professed to "love" him. Her decision to marry him had been based on more practical concerns, such as compatibility and respect. This inherited tendency towards rationality, so evident in Lewis himself too, was very much evident in his decision to marry Joy (and convince an ordained friend to join them in Christian marriage, too, though the Church did not recognize remarriage after divorce), but was overpowered by the tidal wave of grief Lewis felt after his wife's death. He reverted to keeping his emotions close.

The book he published after Joy's death, *A Grief Observed*, is written in pseudonyms and abbreviations, as though Lewis was attempting to push the sorrow away. The loss did more than surprise him with grief; it challenged Lewis' ability to hold onto faith. In *A Grief Observed,* he reveals his anger by asking "Where is God?...Go to him when your need is desperate, when all other help is in vain, and what do you find? A door slammed in your face." When Flora, his mother, had died despite his prayers, young Jack had felt a nothingness when God took her anyway; the passionate response incited by losing Joy reveals how deeply Lewis had allowed himself to love, both his wife and his God. Wrestling with questions of faith was never a one-time event in life; like cancer, they sometimes came back.

The Story Lives On

On November 22, 1963, Lewis died at home, the same day President John F. Kennedy was assassinated in Dallas, Texas; Aldous Huxley also died that same day. Lewis had had a heart attack several months earlier, followed by bouts of intermittent dementia, though in a moment of lucidity in the hospital he greeted a visitor with a reply that shows a deep, unbreakable bond with imagination. Mrs. Moore's adult daughter Maureen, who had inherited a Scottish estate and title from a distant relative, came to the hospital to visit and took Lewis' hand, expecting that she would not be recognized. Lewis denied that she was Maureen, called her by her recently inherited title of Lady Dunbar of Hempriggs, and asked the astonished woman "How could *I* forget a fairy tale?"

And the fairy tale of Lewis' pen lives on. Narnia itself ends with a beginning, as the wild diversity of creatures enters the New Narnia, the old land they once knew fading and falling away like melted snow. "I have come home at last!" a unicorn shouts, in *The Last Battle*. "This is the land I have been looking for all my life, though I never knew it till now." But the journey to such a place "does not begin in comfort," he invites us to remember in *Mere Christianity*, "it begins in dismay." Lewis adds there, though, that the "Christian religion is, in the long run, a thing of unspeakable comfort."

For one whose acceptance of Christianity was described in a hastily scrawled note to a publisher as "an almost purely philosophical conversion," Lewis does seem to have taken faith to heart, living by a standard of kindness and encouragement to his students and to his writer friends, of devotion to those he cared about, and of a determination to forward the essential message of faith by all means, even when it meant admitting the flaws in one's own character and mindset; conceding that some things could never be fully explained; a surrender of control; and risk of awkwardness within family or community. Faith, as he wrote about it, was as unique to each individual, a natural reflection of the multitudinous parts of the body of Christ; God spoke to everyone via their own story, and Lewis' story was certainly unique. As Aslan the lion explains in the fifth book of Narnia, *The Horse and His Boy*, "Child…I am telling you your story, not [someone else's.] I tell no one any story but his own."

"And for us this is the end of all the stories," Lewis offers in *The Last Battle,* "and we can most truly say that they [the Narnians] all lived happily ever after. But for them it was only the beginning of the real story. All their life in this world and all their adventures in Narnia had only been the cover and the title page: now at last they were beginning Chapter One of the Great Story, which no one on earth has read: which goes on for ever: in which every chapter is better than the one before."

Chapter Excerpt from Pope Francis: Pastor of Mercy

If you enjoyed C.S. Lewis: A Life Inspired, you might also enjoy our original biography of Pope Francis, entitled Pope Francis: Pastor of Mercy. Please enjoy the first two chapters on the following pages.

Introduction

There is something about Pope Francis that captivates and delights people, even people who hardly know anything about him. He was elected in only two days of the conclave, yet many who tried their hand at speculating on who the next pope may be barely included him on their lists. The evening of Wednesday, March 13, 2013, the traditional white smoke poured out from the chimney of the Sistine Chapel and spread throughout the world by way of television, Internet, radio, and social media, signaling the beginning of a new papacy. As the light of day waned from the Eternal City, some 150,000 people gathered watching intently for any movement behind the curtained door to the loggia of St. Peter's. A little after 8:00 p.m., the doors swung open and Cardinal Tauran emerged to pronounce the traditional and joyous Latin formula to introduce the new Bishop of Rome: "Annuncio vobis gaudium magnum; habemus papam!" ("I announce to you a great joy: we have a pope!") He then announced the new Holy Father's identity: "Cardinalem Bergoglio..."

The name Bergoglio, stirred up confusion among most of the faithful who flooded the square that were even more clueless than the television announcers were, who scrambled to figure out who exactly the new pope was. Pausing briefly, Cardinal Tauran continued by announcing the name of the new pope, he said "...qui sibi nomen imposuit Franciscum" ("who takes for himself the name Francis"). Whoever this man may be, his name choice resonated with all, and the crowd erupted with jubilant cheers. A few moments passed before the television announcers and their support teams informed their global audiences that the man who was about to walk onto the loggia dressed in white was Cardinal Jorge Mario Bergoglio, age 76, of Buenos Aires, Argentina.

To add to the bewilderment and kindling curiosity, when the new pope stepped out to the thunderous applause of the crowd in St. Peter's Square, he did not give the expected papal gesture of outstretched arms. Instead, he gave only a simple and modest wave. Also, before giving his first apostolic blessing, he bowed asking the faithful, from the least to the greatest, to silently pray for him. These acts were only the beginning of many more words and gestures, such as taking a seat on the bus with the cardinals, refusing a pope mobile with bulletproof glass, and paying his own hotel bill after his election, that would raise eyebrows among some familiar with papal customs and delight the masses.

Is he making a pointed critique of previous pontificates? Is he simply posturing a persona to the world at large to make a point? The study of the life of Jorge Mario Bergoglio gives a clear answer, and the answer is no. This is simply who he is as a man and as a priest. The example of his thought provoking gestures flows from his character, his life experiences, his religious vocation, and his spirituality. This book uncovers the life of the 266th Bishop of Rome, Jorge Mario Bergoglio, also known as Father Jorge; a name he preferred even while he was an archbishop and cardinal.

What exactly do people find so attractive about Pope Francis? Aldo Cagnoli, a layman that developed a friendship with the Pope when he was serving as a cardinal, shares the following: "The greatness of the man, in my humble opinion lies not in building walls or seeking refuge behind his wisdom and office, but rather in dealing with everyone judiciously, respectfully, and with humility, being willing to learn at any moment of life; that is what Father Bergoglio means to me" (as quoted in Ch. 12 of Pope Francis: Conversations with Jorge Bergoglio, previously published as La Jesuita [The Jesuit]).

At World Youth Day 2013, in Rio de Janeiro, Brazil, three million young people came out to praise and celebrate Pope Francis. Doug Barry, from EWTN's Life on the Rock, interviewed youth at the event on what features stood out to them about Pope Francis. The young people seemed most touched by his authenticity. One young woman from St. Louis said, "He really knows his audience. He doesn't just say things to say things... And he is really sincere and genuine in all that he does." A friend agreed: "He was looking out into the crowd and it felt like he was looking at each one of us...." A young man from Canada weighed in: "You can actually relate to [him]... for example, last night he was talking about the World Cup and athletes." A young woman added, "I feel he means what he says... he practices what he preaches... he states that he's there for the poor and he actually means it."

The Holy Spirit guided the College of Cardinals in its election of Pope Francis to meet the needs of the Church following the historic resignation of Pope Benedict XVI due to old age. Representing the growth and demographic shift in the Church throughout the world and especially in the Southern Hemisphere, Pope Francis is the first non-European pope in almost 1,300 years. He is also the first Jesuit pope. Pope Francis comes with a different background and set of experiences. Both as archbishop and as pope, his flock knows him for his humility, ascetic frugality in solidarity with the poor, and closeness. He was born in Buenos Aires to a family of Italian immigrants, earned a diploma in chemistry, and followed a priestly vocation in the Jesuit order after an experience of God's mercy while receiving the sacrament of Reconciliation. Even though he is known for his smile and humor, the world also recognize Pope Francis as a stern figure that stands against the evils of the world and challenges powerful government officials, when necessary.

The Church he leads, is one that has been burdened in the West by the aftermath of sex abuse scandals and increased secularism. It is also a Church that is experiencing shifting in numbers out of the West and is being challenged with religious persecution in the Middle East, Asia, and Africa. The Vatican that Pope Francis has inherited is plagued by cronyism and scandal. This Holy Father knows, however, that his job is not merely about numbers, politics, or even success. He steers clear of pessimism knowing that he is the vicar of the Body of Christ and works with grace. This is the man God has chosen in these times to lead his flock.

Early Life in Argentina

Jorge Mario Bergoglio was born on December 17, 1936, in the Flores district of Buenos Aires. The district was a countryside locale outside the main city during the nineteenth century and many rich people in its early days called this place home. By the time Jorge was born, Flores was incorporated into the city of Buenos Aires and became a middle class neighborhood. Flores is also the home of the beautiful Romantic-styled Basilica of San José de Flores, built in 1831, with its dome over the altar, spire over the entrance, and columns at its facade. It was the Bergoglios's parish church and had much significance in Jorge's life.

Jorge's father's family had arrived in Argentina in 1929, immigrating from Piedimonte in northern Italy. They were not the only ones immigrating to the country. In the late nineteenth century, Argentina became industrialized and the government promoted immigration from Europe. During that time, the land prospered and Buenos Aires earned the moniker "Paris of the South." In the late nineteenth and early twentieth centuries waves of immigrants from Italy, Spain, and other European countries came off ships in the port of Buenos Aires. Three of Jorge's great uncles were the first in the family to immigrate to Argentina in 1922 searching for better employment opportunities after World War I. They established a paving company in Buenos Aires and built a four-story building for their company with the city's first elevator. Jorge's father and paternal grandparents followed the brothers in order to keep the family together and to escape Mussolini's fascist regime in Italy. Jorge's father and grandfather also helped with the business for a time. His father, Mario, who had been an accountant for a rail company in Italy, provided similar services for the family business (Cardinal Bergoglio recalls more on the story of his family's immigration and his early life in Ch. 1 of Conversations with Jorge Bergoglio).

Providentially, the Bergoglios were long delayed in liquidating their assets in Italy; forcing them to miss the ship they planned to sail on, the doomed Pricipessa Mafaldai, which sank off the northern coast of Brazil before reaching Buenos Aires. The family took the Giulio Cesare instead and arrived safely in Argentina with Jorge's Grandma Rosa. Grandma Rosa wore a fur coat stuffed with the money the family brought with them from Italy. Economic hard times eventually hit Argentina in 1932 and the family's paving business went under, but the Bergoglio brothers began anew.

Jorge's father, Mario, met his mother Regina at Mass in 1934. Regina was born in Argentina, but her parents were also Italian immigrants. Mario and Regina married the following year after meeting. Jorge, the eldest of their five children, was born in 1936. Jorge fondly recalls his mother gathering the children around the radio on Sunday afternoons to listen to opera and explain the story. A true porteño, as the inhabitants of the port city of Buenos Aires are called, Jorge liked to play soccer, listen to Latin music, and dance the tango. Jorge's paternal grandparents lived around the corner from his home. He greatly admired his Grandma Rosa, and keeps her written prayer for her grandchildren with him until this day. Jorge recalls that while his grandparents kept their personal conversations in Piedmontese, Mario chose mostly to speak Spanish preferring to look forward rather than back. Still, Jorge grew up speaking both Italian and Spanish.

Upon entering secondary school at the age of thirteen, his father insisted that Jorge begin work even though the family, in their modest lifestyle, was not particularly in need of extra income. Mario Bergoglio wanted to teach the boy the value of work and found several jobs for him during his adolescent years. Jorge worked in a hosiery factory for several years, as a cleaner and at a desk. When he entered technical school to study food chemistry, Jorge found a job working in a laboratory. He worked under a woman that always challenged him to do his work thoroughly. He remembers her, though, with both fondness and sorrow. Years later, she was kidnapped and murdered along with members of her family because of her political views during the Dirty War, a conflict in the 1970's and 80's between the military dictatorship and guerrilla fighters where thousands of Argentineans disappeared.

Initially unhappy with his father's decision to make him work, Jorge recalls later in his life that work was a valuable formative experience for him that taught him responsibility, realism, and how the world operated. He learned that a person's self worth often comes from their work, which led him to become committed later in life to promote a just culture of work rather than simply encouraging charity or entitlement. He believes that people need meaningful work in order to thrive. During his boyhood through his priestly ministry, he experienced the gulf in Argentina between the poor and the well off, which left the poor having few opportunities for gainful employment.

At the age of twenty-one, Jorge became dangerously ill. He was diagnosed with severe pneumonia and cysts. Part of his upper right lung was removed, and each day Jorge endured the pain and discomfort of saline fluid pumped through his chest to clear his system. Jorge remembers that the only person that was able to comfort him during this time was a religious sister who had catechized him from childhood, Sister Dolores. She exposed him to the true meaning of suffering with this simple statement: "You are imitating Christ." This stuck with him, and his sufferings during that time served as a crucible for his character, teaching him how to distinguish what is important in life from what is not. He was being prepared for what God was calling him to do in life, his vocation.

32305143R00075

Made in the USA
Lexington, KY
14 May 2014